THE BUSINESS THAT RUNS ON ITS OWN

10 Steps to Working with a Business Coach That Takes Your Business to the Next Level and Fulfills Your Dream Lifestyle

This book was written by Suresh Iyengar, Profitability Coach, www.buexecution.com
email: suresh.iyengar@buexecution.com

ACKNOWLEDGEMENTS

Thank you to my full circle of friends, family, business colleagues, clients, and others who helped me take the leap in writing this book. It is your support and encouragement that has helped me explore what to highlight in this book. You asked me every step of the way if I had finished writing the book. That kept me going. I'm grateful to you for following up with me.

To the scores of business owners reading this, I salute you.

You have not stopped chasing your dreams. You have relentlessly adapted to the market. You have taken every bold step in growing your business. Your entrepreneurial spirit inspires others to follow in your path to success. Keep up the momentum. There are still more people watching you.

I stand with you on your journey.

TABLE OF CONTENTS

RESOURCES

- Watch your free training at: bit.ly/business-on-autopilot
- Download your free eBook on Big 5 Mistakes in Business Growth at: bit.ly/profitability-coach-houston
- Get your free 25-minute coaching call at: bit.ly/business-unit-execution
- Get your small business evaluation at: bit.ly/small-business-evaluation-survey

PREFACE

You know how we start off in a different way in our career and then move on to develop our skills. That happened to me too. Some people wouldn't hesitate a bit when they talk about me and characterize me as a typical project manager. That was then. Now, I see myself differently. I've developed interest in helping people grow and businesses prosper. And by the way, that became my tag line for my business. It works well because that work is exactly what excites me.

I help business owners achieve their dreams when it comes to their business. It all starts from discovering the areas that are holding them back. Some of my clients have grown their revenues three times in just a year. Many have improved their internal methods, where they now find themselves suddenly attracting more customers—they are now a magnet in their industry. Importantly, business owners find more time in their life after we start working on the business—time outside of their business—time they never had before. That's what they want deep down.

But you might pause for a moment and ask what brought me here. Why first did I become a profitability coach for businesses? What inspired me? Was it serendipity?

To understand, let's rewind.

On that cold winter day in November 2005, I was on a stupendous trip from Houston to Jordan—a less turbulent part of the mid-east. At least, that's what they told me. That wasn't true. And you are about to find out why.

It was official. I was an ambitious project manager for a Fortune 500 company. I was traveling for a UN project for Iraq. It was to automate Iraq's electric power center. All was well—except we were at war at that time. We were at war with an enemy who had no country. We were at war to stop more wars. It all seemed like we were doing the wrong stuff perfectly.

As all of us do, I did what the majesty of the corporate world asked of me. However, I asked questions before travel. I wrote emails. I asked about Jordan's risk level. It was the norm to look at risks. And they told me, "It's business as usual. We are clear to go now."

I didn't feel right–it felt like an unusual start. It was my inner voice.

On a KLM double-decker flight, I was on the window seat. I had no room for my carryon. Overhead cabins were full because the flight was full. So, the attractive flight attendant, dressed in brilliant blue, briskly pushed it where you'd see coats hanging. Next, I eased myself bumping into a couple of heavy folks.

"Excuse me, excuse me...you mind?" I said, as I kept moving. There was just enough room for me to squeeze my legs to reach my seat. I parked myself, but not for long. Scanty air in the plane as people boarded made me uneasy. Now, the attendant helped me trade seats. I went to the aisle.

I asked for something to reduce my uneasiness. I almost wanted to throw up. As the plane jostled the air on takeoff, the flight attendant held her balance, while handing me a quick pill. Instantly, it calmed me.

I didn't know if it was her face or the pill. All the same, I slept through the flight.

Eight hours later, I was in Amsterdam for the day. I booked a small room inside the airport. I had a quick shower and took a nap for about 2 hours.

Just like everybody else, I walked the airport until my legs burned out. Before I knew it, it was time for the flight to Jordan. I reached Amman. An official with a thick mustache behind bulletproof windows stamped a loud seal on my passport. I paid the fee, got my luggage, and took the taxi to the hotel.

"Room 1205 on the 12th floor," the receptionist said, handing me a white card—the key to the room. "Elevators are to the right. Good night, sir," he said.

Soon after I got to the room, my colleague from Sweden showed up. He was tall and lanky. You could tell he walked a few miles a day, like they do in that country. He handed me a big round pill when he found out I felt feverish.

I dropped it in a glass of water. It fizzed. I drank it and I felt better. It worked. As our project team got ready to leave the hotel for dinner, I started to close my door and leave for the cafeteria on the main floor. Just then, Per Amrén stopped me. That may sound like a strange name. To me, that was the name of an Angel. He stopped me from going to the cafeteria and advised me on how I could order the food so I could get it in my room. A second miracle took place that night. You know what it's like when you listen to advice and then follow it. It saved my life, as you are about to find out.

Right after I started on my vegetarian meal, I heard a loud shatter. It felt like an earthquake. The floor shook for a moment. I called the receptionist. It took just an instant. "It was a small kitchen gas tank explosion...nothing to worry about," he replied. I knew it was something bigger. Instantly, news flared on CNN as I switched the TV on.

Two suicide bombers, a husband and wife, exploded in the cafeteria of the hotel, killing more than 60 and injuring more than a 100. Of all events, it was a wedding. The bride and the groom's parents died on the spot. Love turned to horror. Sounds of women wailing in the parking lot filled the air. Lights from police and ambulances lit up the whole area. Smell from smoke rose to the 12th floor of the hotel and beyond.

You know what it feels like when you know you survived a major event. As you sink in your chairs reading this book, picture it vicariously. Many were not that fortunate that night.

This is the reason I call it my second life. Now you know what I mean when I say learn to listen.

I knew I had much more to do in this life. I'm here now before you. Sometimes, you know how you feel, like you are now a ghost. I feel that each time I remember the incident.

When I returned after a couple of days from my trip, reuniting with my parents delighted me. I thanked all those people who helped me get back. You and I are on the same page for now.

I want all of you to enjoy each day as if it's the last.

Cherish your loved ones. Listen to advice. It pays to listen. Here, it paid me with my life. I know now—advice can be priceless. It is worth more for what it can do for you than what you pay for it.

Seven years went by. I descended from the corporate world. You know how seniority plays games when it comes to employment. That happened to me too. I decided I wanted to start a business. And the experience of survival and the value of advice weighed heavily on what business I wanted to start.

I decided to offer advice as a coach and build my experience working with business owners.

That's why I'm here today.

I want to transfer my first-hand experience in building and running a business. I know it will give me the greatest fulfillment in my life and I will be eternally grateful for the opportunity.

Introduction:

ARE YOU A GOOD FIT FOR A BUSINESS COACH?

Growing up in an Indian apartment about 600 square feet in all, I was always watching my father work because he had his office with a long table in the same space that held his equipment. He was an unusual entrepreneur building electronic instruments. To me, he was the first one who coined the phrase "work from home" way back then.

He made his living using nothing he learned in college. He had a degree in Chemistry. Astonishingly, it's the same here. I did not use much I learned in college. To be candid, I had to buy new books when I started my business. I gave all other books to the library. And some of the things I learned in college even kept me going in a different direction until I took a turn. Now I develop new services for my business on the fly. Should we call that serendipity? You decide.

I notice today as we brace this confusion with world conflict and pandemics, we want more focus on our lives. We want miracles to get us over the bridge as this invisible enemy surreptitiously attempts to sweep away our future. The effect is we stop taking risks. We stop expanding our potential. We stop growing. I believe we should exactly do the opposite. We should take risks and fail faster so we dust ourselves and become better at something new. I feel that most of us use less than half our potential. I would urge each of you to stop banking on your jobs and start becoming an entrepreneur, even if it means doing it part-time.

Each time I watched my father work, I found he showed relentless focus. He not only built instruments but also wrote and sent out proposals, invoiced for the work and also spent time learning new technology. It wasn't easy in those days. I can only imagine the bureaucracy and delays. You had to build your network. Without knowing the right people, you wouldn't even begin to know who decides in those companies. Talk about knowing sales, marketing, operations, budgeting, planning and much more. It's about wearing many hats at once. All of this made me know the importance of having the best practices and the benefits of repeatable methods.

Starting my business in 2012 fired me up to succeed. I learned to moil away from my father.

After working twenty years in the corporate world and breaking profitability records, I made a shift. It was a great one—big business to small business. I had built precious experience coaching leaders and business owners worldwide. I knew I could use this in helping small businesses. I invested time and money learning how to coach business owners. I built best practices that would be easily repeatable. That meant better software, efficient tools, templates, and much more. I asked questions and sought answers on how to make my own business successful.

In my pursuit of small business growth, I built experience—cold calling, networking, getting referrals, designing graphics, configuring and setting up CRMs, email marketing, building websites, bookkeeping, social media posting, creating brochures, sending printed material, going door to door, speaking at seminars, etc. To be fully transparent, I did pick up a few clients from all of this activity. Importantly, I learned valuable lessons. It was super time-consuming, slow, unpredictable and definitely NOT scalable. I had many setbacks.

Then I decided to build several incomes. Some passive, others active.

First stream: Digital Marketing. For my business, I set up social media presence—used "Google My Business". This helped me attract businesses looking for consultants and coaches. I could talk directly to more potential clients by posting regularly and applying the best practices. That helped search engines easily find my business. It was called search engine optimization or SEO. I landed more phone calls and eventually more clients. I created the Digital Marketing Service and offered it to business owners using the exact lessons I learned in my own business.

Second stream: Bookkeeping. Using Intuit QuickBooks Online or QBO, I was able to structure my accounting books. I earned QBO certification making me a QuickBooks ProAdvisor. Using my own practical experience, I crafted a brand new QuickBooks fixed fee bookkeeping service and offered it to business owners.

Third stream: Website Design. Using a combination of website building tools and WordPress, I developed expertise in creating professional websites. I built my own website using HTML and CSS first and then used WordPress (www.buexecution.com). Once I made the work repeatable, I offered another service for 3-page and 5-page website design. This service specially catered to busy business owners who wanted affordable, professional, responsive, and modern websites done for you completely inside a week. I offered domain, hosting and even maintenance as part of the service.

Fourth stream: Profitability Coaching. Using advanced tools, templates and business solutions in 21 areas of time, team, and money, I offered a service where I coached business owners to apply growth strategies. First, they went through a thorough small business assessment. Then, we ranked the work so they could apply these strategies week after week.

Fifth stream: Small Business Evaluation report for business owners - automated for purchase through my business website.

Sixth stream: Corporate Business Unit Evaluation and performance improvement—also available for purchase through my website.

Seventh stream: Amazon E-Books on business growth available directly from Amazon.com

Now that I have many streams of income and having worked with business owners and CEOs in different industries, I've since overcome those early setbacks. I'll teach you more about how you can overcome such setbacks that blocked me and my clients so you can experience the exact success and total joy in achieving your business results (and even have more time in your life for your family).

It's easy to tell you to make your business profitable or give you the best practices, but it's your inner desire to work on the business and be receptive to advice from a business coach that will help you most in taking you to the next level. This is the reason I wrote this book—so you not only gain from my experience but also discover your own potential to lift your business and create more impact in achieving your dream lifestyle. The more you work on your business, the more prosperous you could become. But, let me caution you. You will not succeed overnight. You might face frustrating moments. You might not even see the benefits in the first month or two. But know that your endurance will find its results.

I believe everything has a purpose. Your desire to pick up this book means you have the desire to learn, to listen, and to adapt. You show that you want to take charge of your business, your life, and your dreams.

Chapter 1:

WHAT BUSINESS HELP DO YOU NEED?

If you find yourself immersed in this book, I know that you are most likely a business owner, founder, CEO, or entrepreneur who wants rapid business growth. You want answers. You want a different approach. An approach where you learn to work on your business, where you can effectively build quick success but you have to know how to get the right help from the right source so it works for you.

Sadly, few owners recognize the importance of stepping away and looking at the business from the top. What that means is improving procedures in every area of time, team, and money. Research suggests that 50% of businesses fail in the first five years. More than 70% become extinct in the first ten years. When you see the reasons, you will find that it is poor budgeting and cash flow, improper marketing, no bookkeeping or accounting, misaligned teams, and bad strategy. Changing course is about improving procedures. It is about new workflows. Most business owners are busy working in the business—day in and day out. They lack the focus, desire or energy to get a helicopter view. That's the state of mind.

If you want to improve your cash flow, align your team or even fit the right strategy, invest in working on the business. Your work must include the right tools, templates, and the best practices so you can not only automate procedures but also make them repeatable and scalable. Importantly, you have to learn to listen. Be ready to read and digest successful practices in growth. All this takes time.

Moments from now, you might jump back into your business and start the daily grind. That's not the intent of this book. Instead, its purpose is to immerse you in the experience and benefit of building procedures for your business. It is to encourage thought and learning. It is to inspire you to seek out help. But this is no ordinary help. It is coaching and support that could take you and your business to the next level.

Working on your business procedures with advice from a business coach could help you in more than one way. It could help you find freedom you deserve in your business and life.

Time to rewind. It was June 2010. It was hot in Houston, Texas. For some reason, it seemed hotter than normal. I got into my suburban office that early morning. Remember that this was the large electrical engineering company, where I had been working for 13 years in a project management role. Suddenly, I had a phone call from HR. She told me that it was going to be my last day at work.

This is what happened next. I closed my eyes. I could see someone walk up to me. That person had a sticker in her hand. She stuck it on my forehead. It read "worth $0." You know by now that no such thing had really happened, but that's how I felt. It was deep and painful.

But there was good news. I found out that this was the turning point in my life. That helped me re-adjust. I had been under some financial stress because we were expecting our twins the following year. My wife and I worked around it with the severance package. We stretched it a few more months.

I knew that this had become normal for many companies to lay off people. It was especially true after the 2008 crisis. It seemed convenient. Many companies effectively used the crisis for their narrative. I realized that once you reach your forties and fifties, companies find you to be expensive. You could be adding outstanding value. But that does not matter. It had nothing to do with performance. It had all to do with you becoming expensive. And all to do with the company culture.

Within a few months of leaving the job behind, I started my own company. I decided on a name and even a tag line. I wanted to still help the company I had left. People who knew me could tell that I wanted to contribute in any way that I could.

In the beginning, I created some business professional courses for project managers. It seemed logical that I would get consulting gigs from the place where I spent so many years of my life. Unfortunately, it did not happen. I took that not as failure but as a challenge. I found the gap. Something had to change. I had to learn to sell my skills in the market. I had to learn to package them. I had to invest in becoming smarter in sales and marketing. I knew I never had the chance to explore these areas because I had already earned the stereotype of a technology project manager. That's how it mostly works when you are an employee. And I no longer wanted to be in that state.

Now, I have to be frank. I did not give up applying for jobs altogether. However, I did not pin my hopes on fitting into the political structure of most companies. I wanted a flexible working style where I could use my creative skills and make a big return on the company's investment. You might notice that I was already thinking and talking in the language of an entrepreneur. I even explored franchises, but I didn't like the idea of royalties. Especially, when most of them did not invest or commit to your success in sales.

That's what brought me to become a business coach. I wanted to work for myself. I knew I could gather my vast skills not only in working with top executives but also my abilities in making businesses profitable. I knew how to work with customers and vendors. I understood contracts. I had a strong project management DNA. I'm certified in different fields. To complement, I already had experience in advanced software tools such as SAP. I had the full package—ready to go.

However, I knew there was one missing area. There was one skill where I knew I could make a bigger impact if I mastered it. The language of sales. I invested in learning neuro linguistic programming or NLP. It was pleasantly surprising to know that this skill could help me with more than just sales. It transformed my life. Importantly, it helped me phrase better questions that opens minds. And that means so much when you talk about coaching business owners.

Most people don't invest in a business coach because of imaginary reasons. They don't see what they are losing when they don't achieve the full stretch for their business or when they don't apply best practices or even when they don't have anyone to keep them accountable for their own success. Working on your business could free up more time in your routine, increase your profits and even align your teams so they treat your business as if it's their own.

What if you could delegate your work using a defined method so you recover your time from the business? What if you could have customers chase your business when you have a well-crafted unique selling point for your goods and services? What about setting the perfect key performance indicators for your employees so they know exactly how their work improves your business results? These are just a few examples. There is so much more you could learn when you work on your business.

At the moment, you might find the idea of working on the business as new and maybe you might feel this isn't you. But by the end of this book, you will have a richer experience. Whether you use the ideas I present here or not, you will move one step closer to more growth in your business. That's exactly what I intend to give my readers. One thing you are going to find out when you work with me is when you find out how easily you can carry out the strategies I offer your business, because you get support and objective advice, support that is timely, support that is practical, support that will drastically reduce resistance helping you get through the decisions that will make your business growth even more effective. That's the journey you and I will make when you join one of my programs.

UNCONSCIOUS BIAS

Some business owners have an unconscious bias when they decide to work with business coaches. They fear their employees will notice that their leader has flaws. Thus, they'll believe that to be the reason he works with a coach.

Allow me to dispel the myth.

Coaching is not to fix problems. It is to expand your abilities to go beyond your self-imposed limits. It is to help you solve problems in a way that is repeatable and sustainable. It is to change your mindset about business growth and know what's possible.

When I was cold calling, one business owner had this to say, "I've been in this business for 30 years. Do you think I need a coach? What makes you an expert in my business?"

I had to pause and then I replied in this way, "You will remain an expert in your business. I won't change that. But I will offer you help in making your business more profitable and scalable." This business owner did not become my client for obvious reasons but then I also did not want to work with someone who isn't ready for possibilities and change.

CONSULTANT OR COACH

There is a difference between hiring a consultant and hiring a business coach.

A consultant solves a specific business problem you define, charges by the hour and leaves.

A coach, on the other hand, offers you advice, support and guidance and works with you week after week until you achieve your goals. It is a combination of achieving the full potential of your business, offering tools, best practices and strategies, then keeping you accountable for your own success.

You have to decide what type of help you need for your business.

WHEN MARKETING IS A BOTTOMLESS PIT

It's mind-boggling to see so many businesses plan marketing without a budget. It is a blind approach. No return on investment. No measurement of cost per lead. No idea how far to spend before they win a client or customer.

That's a mistake.

When I work with my clients, we begin with a marketing plan. We look at different channels and set up ways to measure the number of inbound leads from each channel. Then we refine our funnels so we can get a close estimate of our cost per lead. We also focus on outbound activity. However, I favor a strong inbound marketing strategy.

Marketing should never become a bottomless pit

WHY SALES CONVERSION NEEDS THREE STEPS

Have you wondered what takes place when a customer decides to buy your goods or services? What are the thoughts that go through their mind before they take action? The answers to these questions will bring you closer to the three steps we need to make a sale.

Step 1: Approach

An approach to selling means you paint a picture of the future experience. Think of what your customer will see, hear or feel after owning your product or service. Importantly, this needs more provocative questions, where you could ferret out the real pain or needs. It only stays as wants until you convert them into needs.

Step 2: Skills

When you develop skills, it is about polishing four areas. First, you build trust with the client. That means you earn the right to the next conversation. Second, you uncover the need and earn the right to the next conversation. Third, you help the client by adding value. Fourth, you explain the benefit the customer will experience if they go forward with your goods and services.

Step 3: Attitude

Sales isn't easy when you take it out of the box. It needs a change in attitude. Tricks and tactics of deception do not live long. They fail once the customer figures out you aren't trustworthy. Even worse outcome is when they will never ever return to work with you. Ouch! That's painful.

WHAT SHOULD YOU DO THEN?

Build powerful phrases that help overcome negative thoughts. You could even replace your thoughts about your inability to sell with no bad habits to unlearn. That's only a start. Repeat these phrases often. Your subconscious state will help you reframe the past for your client. And that will pave the way for your next sale.

FORESIGHT IN FINANCE AND OPERATIONS

One of the most value-added steps we first take when you join the coaching program is when you fill out the one page finance sheet. Using your own estimates with coaching help, we project more than 50% increase in bottom line profits. You will then notice right away that coaching pays itself off only within a few months. That's the guaranteed benefit I offer when we work together.

The ability to forecast the effect of applying strategies influences the growth of your company.

For example, setting up key performance indicators for your teams or applying the cash flow plan will improve the finance ratios that define the health of your business.

When you install a performance incentive plan, set up an organization structure or carry out a strategic plan, your team will improve operations in a way that they work together and pull your company forward together.

When I work with business owners, we review various metrics in each coaching session. This includes monthly revenue and profit goals, actual revenues and profits, leads, sales conversion, revenue per client and profit margins.

The reason we take up this task is because it builds foresight and discipline in driving the business to pre-defined goals.

DELEGATION TO UNCOVER ROLES AND RESPONSIBILITIES

Some business owners cannot extract themselves from the daily churn in their business. One of the easiest ways they could relieve themselves from certain types of work is by using a delegation plan.

But what is a delegation plan and what work should you assign to others?

A delegation plan helps you transfer low-value tasks to your team so you could focus on other tasks that produce revenue.

We work together on four stages to train the delegated team member. You perform the task while they watch and then help. Next, they do the task while you help and then finally watch.

When you are able to watch them do the task, it means you are ready for transferring the task.

By transferring the right tasks to the right people from your organization, you can find more time for tasks that help you accelerate your business growth.

TIME TROUBLE

The biggest issue owners face is a "catch -22" situation. You have no time for coaching because you are running out of time working in the business. You are running out of time in your business because you have no time for coaching. It's a vicious circle.

The whole idea of profitability coaching is to extract your valuable time from your business through a time recovery plan. It helps you place your highest value activities on your calendar and makes you accountable to yourself.

That's what we do when we work together on your business.

KEY TAKEAWAYS

- Work with the right business coach to raise your business level
- Working with a business coach is about learning and development
- Know the difference between a business consultant and coach
- Foresight in finance & operations for reaching defined goals
- Delegate and uncover roles and responsibilities
- Extract time for yourself by working on the business

Chapter 2:

HAVE THIS IN PLACE BEFORE YOU APPROACH A COACH

When I started in my coaching business, I worked hard on the tools and methods that would help me talk clearly about the benefits of coaching. After all, that is the service I was about to offer.

I built a presentation to help business owners discover ways to grow their business. Next, I prepared a workbook that they could fill out with takeaways from the meeting.

All the planning took time. I wrote the event description and posted it on Eventbrite, a software that helps publish the schedule and meeting details. I posted three weeks before the meeting. It made sense. I thought it would give people time to join.

I held these meetings at a local bank. They had an elegant meeting room. And they didn't even charge for it, but I had to book in advance. That wasn't the issue. It could house about 12 people at most. Even that worked for me.

Here is what happened. Three weeks went by and I had just two people sign up for the event. Yet, I stayed hopeful. At least, if one of them joined my coaching program, it would still be worth the effort. That's what I figured. But it didn't go as planned.

Of the two people who signed up, one showed up. I did the presentation. We exchanged cards. But there was no sale.

It frustrated me, especially after all the planning and effort. It felt like a thankless activity. I knew I was offering outstanding value in my coaching services. However, the message wasn't reaching the right audience. I had to change my plan. I found out that I needed more traffic, interested prospects and sales conversion. I had to invest more money in advertising or networking.

I adopted a new strategy. I talked with more business owners and invited them for the next presentation. I had to get in front of people. It worked.

My next presentation was a packed house. I did it in the local library and had more than 20 people.

There was excitement and interest. I had more people wanting to know about my signature coaching program. Everything looked good and ready, except there was another glitch. We were hit with the pandemic. Many businesses had to change their models. They went from brick and mortar to online. I had to also adapt to the needs of the market. That took another step back. But I kept at it. I did not lose heart.

From these experiences, I realized the importance of working on the business. It is vital that we apply a winning strategy for business growth and cut the cycle of lost time using unproven methods. That's what I sharpened. I want to transfer the exact same success to you.

Now, I have expanded my business services. Each one adds terrific value to your business. Whether it is lead generation from social media,

QBO bookkeeping, digital marketing or ever website design, you will get ahead sooner because I have the tools, methods and proven strategies. I even tested them successfully. We can now easily tailor them to fit your business.

The more you know about these services, the more you will begin to discover exactly how I could help you cut through the chase to rapid growth.

However, you need to check if you are ready in these 7 areas before you start working with a business coach.

DESIRE TO WORK ON THE BUSINESS

The more desire you have to work on the business, the more you will benefit from working with a business coach.

It shows you are willing to carve out time away from the business to talk about the way you carry out each task. And that also means you have an interest in finding out different ways or better ways of doing the same work.

Some business owners compare others who take help from business coaches and focus on the results they achieved. However, they often ignore the journey you have to take so you make it to your final destination.

It's not just about the glory of success but also the struggle and the perseverance through that struggle that makes the difference.

Because business owners find themselves busy during the day, I set up meetings with them on the weekends. It gives a clear message when a person who wants to work on his business during the weekend is more likely to show interest in working on the business. That would make him a good candidate for business coaching.

People who do not believe in strategic thinking would find the idea of working on the business untenable. They lose focus and will not see value in working with a business coach or mentor.

That is the reason I pick my clients carefully so we make best use of our time. It is clearly the best recipe for your success.

TIME INVESTMENT

How much time do you have to invest so you grow your business in 6 months? It depends. The size of your business, the number of employees, the industry, the economic conditions and even the business model are some of the factors.

It is clear.

If you are the CEO or entrepreneur or business owner, time is precious. That is why spending time on the business is even more important. It could change the way you work. You could get away from your daily hustle.

If you believe you don't have time to work on the business, then I'd say don't even bother hiring a business coach.

Depending on the program, you will need to invest between 5 and 20 hours each week working on the business to see your business effectively grow.

That includes the time you spend in coaching sessions and the time you take carrying out various strategies from those sessions.

There is no short cut.

MONEY INVESTMENT

Whether you hire a consultant or a coach, you know you will have to invest money? That's a given.

If it is a consultant, it could be an hourly rate. You probably sign off first on a proposal. Your return of investment here depends on how you evaluate the work and business results you achieve from the work the consultant does.

If it is a business coach, you could expect a monthly fee depending on the number of times you meet each month. For example, I offer a Bronze-level coaching program where I meet for about an hour and a half, twice a month.

Before we start on the program, I do a finance exercise with my client.

We take their past year performance and I show them how their finance numbers could change in five areas based on the business solutions I offer in those areas. Interestingly, the client is the one who estimates the percentage growth in each area. They do it based on their belief in the effectiveness of the solution strategies I present.

That's the power of the business coaching program I offer.

Those clients who have benefited from it vouch on its ability to help them grow their business faster than ever before.

CLEAR ACCOUNTING BOOKS

This might startle you. I was doing my round of cold calls. When I called one business owner to enlist him for profitability coaching, he declined. Before I could hang up, he stopped me and asked if I could help him sell his furniture business.

Naturally, I wanted to know how he came up with the price that he expected from the sale. He had no answer. Then he revealed some more. He had no bookkeeping or accounting books because he did not believe in paying a bookkeeper or CPA for keeping the books.

You probably guessed it right by now. I couldn't help him and had to hang up the phone.

There are many other businesses in this condition, where they have no accounting books

They don't yet understand that cash in the bank is not cash flow in your business. That's why they can never grow.

There are several benefits of having clear accounting books. It therefore pays to hire a fixed fee bookkeeper for your business. First, you can see the health of your business any time, or from anywhere if you are using QuickBooks online or QBO and have internet.

Once you freeze your past year's books after filing your taxes, you could use your profit and loss report as supporting financial evidence when you apply for a business loan.

You can check your cash flow for your business.

You can check gross margin and improve profitability.

Finally, clear accounting books help increase the value of your business. You could use the last three years of cash flow in a discounted cash flow method to find your business worth.

ONLINE PRESENCE OR WEBSITE

Do not hire a profitability coach if you aren't ready to use your website or online presence to grow your business. That's what I tell business owners who come to my presentation, where I go over the top mistakes in business growth.

There are other untapped areas even after building your website.

For example, make sure you are not missing a funnel. It is a way to offer freebies such as free training or an E-book in exchange for the visitor's name and e-mail address.

If you are offering consultations, it is pressing to have a scheduling button right on the menu.

Having a website helps finding new customers, building trust, saving time, saving money, preventing bad reviews and increasing profits.

You are leaving money on the table if you don't have a website working for you.

That's why I focused on eliminating procrastination for business owners by offering them a "done-for-you" 3-page or 5-page professional website inside one week.

ABILITY TO APPLY SUGGESTED STRATEGIES

If you are working with a business coach, what does it take for you to succeed? Your ability to apply suggested strategies in the areas of time, team and money.

You may be one who is ready and able to do it. However, there are some business owners who cringe when they have to take risks. Every strategy is a change.

If you embrace change, it will be easy to get ahead. If you resist, it gets harder to change outcomes.

That's why having the ability to apply strategies also needs the right mindset. We will talk more about that in the next chapter.

DESIRE TO REVIEW COMPANY FINANCIAL METRICS

If you have a business, you must like numbers. There's no way around it.

When I use QuickBooks Online, I can see at one glance where my firm stands today. I can use reports for profit and loss or balance sheets to dive deeper. There are even more choices to monitor the business.

Your desire to check your business finance and metrics will help you understand the health of your business. For example, accounts receivables show you uncollected funds from customers, accounts payables show you what you owe your suppliers, gross margin shows how much profit you are earning on your goods and services and debt ratios highlight your liquidity.

57

If you want to compare your business with other businesses in your zip code, you could do it using tools such as LivePlan. It offers benchmarking reports. As an Intuit QuickBooks ProAdvisor and LivePlan Expert advisor, I help my clients review their business profitability during each coaching session.

KEY TAKEAWAYS

- Hire a business coach only if you love working on the business
- Working on the business means you need to invest time
- Working with a business coach means investing money
- Set up clear accounting books before working on the business

- Working with a business coach means you believe in using technology and online presence to grow your business
- Applying strategies to grow your business needs right mindset
- Desire to review and learn about business financials is a must if you want to grow your business

Chapter 3:

CHECK FOR MINDSET

There are many ways to look at mindset. It is a compass that guides us to actions. There is one small problem. This compass is driven by a collection of our life experiences. It gives us direction. It may not be the right way to go. Yet, it forms our default viewpoint. It is our default direction.

Now that we know what it is, how do we change direction? Remember, you want to rapidly grow your business. That's why you picked up this book, didn't you? That also means that you aren't getting the growth you want in your business right now. That means change is imminent.

But how should a business owner change?

It depends. If you want a growth mindset, you have to take more risks.

At any moment, you have two choices.

Choice #1: Take risks, work on the business, apply the best practices using objective advice from a business coach.

Choice #2: Continue to work in the business, day in and day out. You continue to get the same results from the work you do.

If you pick Choice #1, you are embracing a "learning experience". That means you are willing to try strategies that help your business grow. Yet, you are aware of the probabilities of success. If it does not succeed, you adjust. You do it until it is exactly what you want from your business growth.

But let me caution you. You may be tested. You may not succeed instantly when you work week after week. You might not even agree with the change that is necessary for your business growth. You might find that your teams reject the approaches when you bring them up. You could even have to find your own answers to your business challenges even when you have the best practices in front of you.

Yet, you know it is within your power to try. And that, I have helped hundreds of other leaders like you succeed using the same proved best practices in the areas of time, team, and money.

When I realized my inner calling is to help people grow and businesses prosper, I could propel my business even more.

You also have to dig deep to figure out your inner calling. If your business solves a challenge for your customers, then you want to do it consistently and in a way that is scalable.

Imagine yourself working fewer hours but more effectively than ever before. You find that your teams treat your business as if it's their own. Your short-term, mid-term, and long-term plans consistently reflect your mission, vision, and core values. Your revenues are up, profits up and fixed costs down. Weekly, you see your teams send you their individual KPIs.

What would all this do for you? If it makes sense, then by all means I'm ready to help. If not, that's okay too. At least you learned something important about yourself.

Here are some areas that are important if one wants to work with a business coach.

PERSONALITY

Let's face it. We are all different. We have our likes, dislikes, beliefs and so much more that is part of who we are. That's what we show the world.

But what if we could mask it, just for a short time while we talk with someone who is completely different.

If we just knew what the other person likes, we could do more of that. If we knew what the other person dislikes, we could avoid it before the relationship turns sour. Imagine if you had a technique that could help you know in advance not only more about others but also more about yourself.

That's exactly what a DISC report shows. DISC stands for dominance, influence, steadiness, and compliance.

When I work with my clients, I help them take the DISC assessment and then we review their results.

Your personality shows if you are fit for coaching. It shows your brand.

What that means is your desire to learn and your ability to listen to advice are vital ingredients that could help you benefit when working with a coach.

Obviously, you also need to follow through on the advice and take action.

In my experience, I see that if one has the belief in learning and self-improvement, that business owner will be extremely successful working with a coach.

Mostly, such business owners may lift their business to the next level.

LISTENING SKILLS

There is no better skill than listening because it helps build relationships.

Whether you are learning from a coach or whether you are talking with your customer, listening plays a big part in both places.

I look for business owners who understand the importance of listening in business.

If I offer strategies for you to carry out, then it is necessary for you to digest it and then ask follow-up questions. That is the way we can make progress in business growth.

Some business owners who work in the business all day find it hard to now listen to someone who is asking questions about their business. The purpose of the question is to open up the conversation and discover the best strategy that could help.

Sometimes we don't have all the answers. That is the time we have to practice even greater listening to find the best solution.

Even when I notice that clients have tried to go the wrong path before joining my program, I compliment their efforts. Their perseverance shows. It is worth praise. I ask the famous question that opens our conversation: "What's most important to you in your business?" That helps them think focus.

I help business owners improve their sales conversations by coaching them on asking better questions. That makes them talk less when they engage with their customers. Yet, it helps strengthen relationships like never before.

When we use surveys or watch for voice or intonation in direct conversations, it is important to notice what is unsaid. It could reveal much more that lies under the iceberg. That could help you improve your goods and services. It is also the reason I favor qualitative surveys more than quantitative ones.

Finally, asking better questions about how someone enjoyed their buying experience could tell you what you could use back in the same conversation. That strengthens rapport.

WHAT OTHERS THINK

To successfully work with a business coach, business owners don't worry about what their employees think.

There is no need to treat coaching as a therapy for a weakness because it is not. When you decide to work with a business coach, it is more about improving your skills and expand your competency in growing your business.

Why then should you even entertain this thought?

After all, you don't see a top tennis player hide in the closet when he announces he'll be working with a new coach to help him improve his game. It is about the game, and even if it is about mindset, it is meant for learning and development. Most often, it is not about erasing a destructive personal habit.

Sometimes the business owner wants to learn and finds outstanding value from coaching, but on hiring an overpowering need, they find it difficult to disclose coaching expenses. This happens when a bully wants transparency to the business financials. Such a person then decides to question all company expenses, acting for the owner. It could be a new employee who considers himself or herself to be a company partner, even if it isn't official.

This is a big mistake.

No owner should ever yield to such asks just because he is dependent on the employee in some way.

In such cases, it works best when owners find their own way to keep the privacy in their coaching engagement.

COMPETING PRIORITIES

Coaching faces competition from other priorities in the business. That is why owners stall coaching meetings. They want to decide after they fight fires so they don't have to postpone these meetings—yet again.

That is when I put the brakes. You have to know that working on the business is as important as the fires you put out daily. Sometimes, it is more important because it will get you out of the firefighting mode. That is also one of the purposes of business coaching.

It takes time and patience for business owners to discover their priorities when they work with me on coaching. But it is time well spent. And it is patience well earned.

PARTNERS AND INTERFERENCE

Some partners may object to coaching or may prefer not to be part of the sessions. Either they feel it is unnecessary or lack the appreciation.

I prefer to work with business owners one-on-one, and if they have another partner or partners, it is their responsibility to tell them that they are part of such coaching sessions.

It is much better to be clear from the start so there is no disruption to the coaching program. As it is a month-to-month engagement, one benefits more when we have a rhythm in carrying out strategies, at least over 3 to 6 months forward. That is when most owners begin to see outstanding value from applying the new strategies.

ACCOUNTABILITY

One of the key benefits of business coaching you will discover is when you are held accountable for your own progress. Most business owners find it difficult to talk with people about their business. And I understand.

That is why talking with your coach helps you steer your business and bring out your innermost concerns and challenges inside your business.

When you are held accountable, it means there is no one to pass the buck. You are the last answerable person for your business.

As your business coach, I stand with you to listen to your business issues and we will work together to carry out the most optimum strategy so you could grow your business than you ever thought possible.

KEY TAKEAWAYS

- Build trust by assessing and adjusting your personality
- Develop listening skills and build better relationships
- Having a business coach on your side expands your learning
- Manage coaching priorities and other needs

- Tell partners about your business coaching commitments
- Keeping you accountable to achieve peak performance is another benefit from business coaching

Chapter 4:

HOW TO DRIVE YOUR BUSINESS TO BECOME A CLIENT MAGNET

Let me guess. Most of you have learned to drive your car one way or another. If you are like me you probably started with a driving school.

I learned to drive my first car in India. You might probably already know the steering wheel is on the right side there and the traffic flows in the opposite direction compared to the USA.

On arriving at the school, I faced a question from my driving coach: "Have you ever driven a car before?"

To that I answered, "No, sir." "What would you like to be able to do after you finish your driving school?"

And I replied: "I want to become competent in driving any car—besides getting a license to drive."

Note there is a difference between competence and skills. I could have skills even if I have never driven on the road. But I will become competent only when I have driven several hours successfully on the road. So, that was my goal.

We agreed. Then, I started my first lesson after signing up.

It was an old Fiat. India had many of those in the '80s. On starting the car, it rattled a bit and had a rhythm to the noise it made. I sat in front of the steering and stared through the glass, looking at what was in front of me. The driving coach sat to my left. He then directed me, "Change from neutral to the first gear." I did. The car started moving and thrilled me.

As I spent more coaching sessions, I became better at driving. It took over a month. Finally, I could drive with little or no help from the coach. I even earned my driver's license. Soon, I earned driving competency.

When I look at what happens when I work with a business owner, it is similar. Except, here we are learning to drive a business. And the goal is to competently drive it. At least, that's what most business owners expect from coaching.

In contrast to becoming a competent auto driver, you discover how to drive your business results. It usually takes longer than learning to drive a car. Yet, the questions your coach will ask you will be strikingly similar.

Your landscape when you drive your business is the presence of other competitors, your dashboard is your QuickBooks online screen, your mileage will become your business expenses your road will be marked by your business profits, and your fuel will be your working capital and cash flow. With no cash flow, your business will stop sooner than later, much like your car with no gas.

Your destination is your business growth, which means your revenue and profit levels.

With the road you have, the car you drive, the landscape in front and the fuel you have left, you could estimate how soon you will reach your destination.

Similarly, with the business you drive, the competitive landscape for your goods and services and the profits and cash flow you produce, you could estimate how soon you could take it to the next level.

That also means that it depends on the strategies you apply compared to others in the market and the lessons you learn working with your coach. Day after day. Week after week. Month after month. Year after year.

WEEKLY COACHING AGENDA

Some business owners realize the value of having the weekly coaching agenda and work towards growing their business. They realize that knowing your revenue goals and profits you intend to make are relevant to sustainable growth.

Other business owners take time to adopt the weekly coaching agenda. Some want to jump into question and answer sessions on the challenges they face in their business.

Either way, I'm ready to help my clients achieve their goals.

However, I find that storing the weekly coaching agenda, listing your goals, making a commitment to achieve them, and discussing the challenges you faced in the past weeks helps me as a coach to understand your situation even better.

The more you discipline yourself to prepare the weekly coaching agenda, the more you will gain from business coaching. And that will take you faster towards your goal to grow your business.

SET REALISTIC GOALS

What are realistic goals? These are goals you could achieve in a reasonable time period. They also cannot be goals outside your total competence.

When I work with clients, we set three or 4 business goals, where we can review them over a week or two week period. Some are easy to finish. Others could take a few more weeks.

The idea of listing them in the coaching agenda helps you become accountable to not only measure the progress but also report them during our coaching sessions.

MONTHLY ACCOUNTING REPORTS

There are two important reports that we could use to drive your business financials. One is the profit and loss report and the other is the balance sheet report. We look at them directly using QuickBooks online.

The purpose of looking at these reports as part of the coaching agenda is to verify the profitability you have achieved in the past month. It also shows the pattern for your revenues and expenses.

Using this dashboard, you could easily target growth for the next month, quarter, and year.

MARKETING STATUS

Did you measure your return on your marketing investment? One of the key steps in making marketing effective is to build a marketing plan. There, we outline the channels we plan to use.

We then look at targeted leads versus actual leads we were able to produce.

When we sum up the marketing cost for the month and then divide out the number of leads, we could then see our cost per lead. We can also evaluate the successful marketing channels and reshuffle the budget to the more productive ones.

These are some of the steps we take during our coaching sessions and review them as part of the coaching agenda.

SALES CONVERSIONS

Your success in converting sales and winning customers depends on your sales conversation, sales scripts and the quality of your marketing leads.

You could certainly improve the lead quality if you have a powerful unique selling point for your business.

Your sales conversation needs to focus on the customer and you have to build your ability to uncover the real reason for buying your goods and services.

In our coaching sessions, we will work on exercises to strengthen and rehearse sales conversation for you and your team using pre-written scripts. This will produce fluency and trust with your customer because they will feel you are confident about your goods and services.

The more you rehearse and prepare your sales procedure, the more sales conversion you can expect.

If you have done these steps and still fall short in the percentage of sales conversion, we will focus on the quality of the marketing lead and a stronger unique selling point.

Combining all these steps in our coaching sessions will uncover outstanding value for your business.

CASH FLOW FORECAST

Forecasting cash flow is an exercise. You look at all the cash outflow minus all the cash inflow over each month. You do it over a period of time.

Your cash inflow is all the cash coming in from sales to your customers, and your cash outflow is the money you pay your suppliers and employees.

Note that cash in the bank at any moment is not the same as cash flow.

And profit is not the same as cash flow cither. Your business may be profitable and yet run out of cash.

That's not desirable.

Therefore, forecasting cash flow is an exercise that every business owner should do. To maintain a positive cash flow, take the following steps:

- Set up net 0 terms so your customers pay on delivery
- Extend terms to pay your supplier bills
- Buy less inventory and keep no inventory, if possible
- Follow up and ask customers to pay up back debts
- Set up a line of credit or other type of business loan

Using QBO, I work with clients where we could connect with LivePlan and review cash flow forecasting.

FOLLOW UP AND TAKE ACTION

Some business owners agree to take action and agree the strategy will work but miss following up and taking action.

Sometimes, it is just the state of mind where they have too many tasks and priorities. They don't have the fire burning in them long enough.

But following up is the cornerstone of carrying out any strategy. You need to be creative in housing changes to any plan.

It is the same when it comes to coaching. Each time we have a coaching session, I'm following up with my client to see how far they have come in achieving their goals. These are the same goals they committed to achieve in their last session.

Follow through also helps align teams in the business because they now believe that you want to carry out that strategy. It is a trait that shows commitment.

Even a meeting held has to be filled with purpose, actions, assignments, dates and again—follow through.

That's when you build it in the company culture to carry out strategies and get results.

KEY TAKEAWAYS

- Realize the importance of weekly coaching agenda
- Set practical goals inside your sphere of competence
- Know the top two monthly accounting reports
- Review marketing return on investment

- Know how to convert sales and how to improve
- Understand cash flow and what it takes to make it positive
- Realize the importance of follow-up, taking action and reporting back

Chapter 5:

CHOOSE YOUR COACH AND MOBILIZE YOUR STRATEGIC PLAN IN 90 DAYS

It was 1988. I spoke English when I entered the United States because I had education in English until then.

That doesn't convey much when you listen to what I found out when I was ready to graduate with a master's degree from the United States.

It was time to leave the school. And I thought of taking the next step.

As it is common practice, I asked my thesis advisor for a letter of recommendation. To that he asked me, "Suresh, who do you want me to address in this letter?"

Remember, I spoke English, but I spoke Indian English. So, I replied in a tone that would imply it's obvious, "To Whomsoever it May Concern."

That startled him, and he retorted, "So, you don't care a rat's ass who I write this letter to. Is that right?"

Naturally, I shuddered a bit. On further research, I found out that in the United States, one would say, "To Whom it May Concern." Just the extra British words got me into trouble that I would never forget. That even taught me a bigger lesson. If just a few words could dislocate our communication, imagine the power of spoken language.

Yet, I'm aware of many others who may have migrated from other countries with little or bare minimum English proficiency. I knew that I had an advantage.

But what would it look like if I had to carry out the strategic plan? I mean a plan that outlines my mission, vision, and core values so all my work takes me forward in my career in the years to come.

Note that here I'm talking about the success using my ability to speak in English and get ahead.

What would be my mission here? It is the goal to become an accomplished communicator so people in the United States understand me and I get the results I expect when I talk with them.

What is my vision? It answers the question why I want people to understand me. If people get what I'm saying, I know that I will advance in my career and get what I want from life in the United States.

- What are my core values? These are the steps I should take to advance my career using my proficiency in the English language:
- That means I should learn to write and speak with absolute clarity. The words I choose should be apt and meaningful. The intonation in the language I use should build stronger personal and work relationships.
- Next, I look at strengths, weaknesses, opportunities and threats. The ability to

understand, write, and read English makes up my strength. The ability to adapt it to American English would make up my opportunities. The use of complex British words would reduce clarity in my communication and would make up my weaknesses. The pronunciations and intonations used differently could make up the threats in my ability to adapt to American life and its environment.

- The ability to write, read, and speak about learning and experiences from a different continent would then make up my unique selling point.

Now let's see how this example could apply to your business growth if you build your strategic plan.

COMPANY MISSION

Your business mission answers the question on what your company does. It gives employees a way to approach their work so they achieve company goals.

The mission also represents your business culture and sets the direction for the future.

COMPANY VISION

Your company vision answers the question on why your company is in business. It is the business dream with a plan. The vision sits on the core values of your company and represents the rules your business follows.

UNIQUE SELLING POINT

The unique selling point is a compelling reason for people to do business with your company and not your competitors because you are different.

That means you have to find your niche and highlight the top three things you do that your competitor doesn't.

With a strong unique selling point, you will lower the pressure on sales to win customers. In a way, it helps your goods and services sell themselves without any pressure or added marketing.

Let me caution you. It takes effort because you are defining your business strategy when you pick your unique selling point.

Some business owners take three to six months to finish their unique selling point. I help them include it in all their content such as their website, brochures and landing pages so everyone knows what you do best. That attracts the right customers to your business.

SWOT (STRENGTHS, WEAKNESSES, OPPORTUNITIES, THREATS) ANALYSIS

When you compete for the market, it is important that you know your strengths, weaknesses, opportunities, and threats (SWOT).

It could change over time, but you have to know at least the top 5 strengths and weaknesses of your business. Evaluating them every quarter will ensure you are competing strong.

Check the top 5 most daunting threats facing your business.

Check also the top 5 opportunities your business could hunt so you could convert them into business results.

Pick a reasonable timeframe to take advantage of these opportunities and countering the threats. That will keep you on the top of your competition.

If clients struggle here, I work with them so they clearly see their strengths, weaknesses, opportunities, and threats.

KPI (KEY PERFORMANCE INDICATOR) METHOD

What is a key performance indicator (KPI) method? It is a procedure, where you measure and report tasks your team performs.

It improves the efficiency of your business operations. Importantly, it helps your team know how their work improves business results and what they need to do to change if it doesn't.

When I work with business owners, I help them identify the best 5 KPIs that they could pick from different areas of their business. It could be marketing, sales, operations, and finance.

Once you do, you could have your team SMS their KPIs to your phone each day or each week so you know your business is moving in the right direction.

QUARTERLY PERFORMANCE

Some business owners wonder how to drive quarterly performance. The best way is to use one number that you use to focus on achieving a single goal.

You could aim for any goal such as "zero defects" or "product launch" or "won 10 new customers" or "20 five-star customer reviews" as an example.

What this does is it inspires your full team to not only translate the strategy but act congruently on achieving results.

When we work together, you will see how we could customize this goal for your business so you align your team for their quarterly performance.

SHORT-TERM, MID-TERM AND LONG-TERM GOALS

Short-term goals show what you plan to do inside 2 years.

When you review annual goals, set 5 or 6 key initiatives. Break them down into 5 or 6 action steps over 3 months. This also defines how you will achieve results. They are different from the day-to-day work. Weekly work deliverables help each team member meet their KPIs more efficiently.

Mid-term goals show what you plan to do from 2 to 5 years. These are 5 or 6 targets that show new capabilities you want to achieve in that time period.

Long-term goals are lofty and define the bigger aims of the company such as dominating an industry or going international.

Working with my coaching clients, I help them outline their strategic plan inside 3 to 6 months. It depends on their progress in developing KPIs, creating a unique selling point and outlining their mission, vision, and core values.

KEY TAKEAWAYS

- Your mission statement answers what your business does.

- Your vision statement answers why your company is in business.

- Your unique selling point is about difference and not superiority.

- Analyze and know your business SWOT.

- Know how to set up a KPI method for your team.

- Have a single goal for measuring quarterly performance.

- Know what your short-term, mid-term, and long-term goals are.

Chapter 6:

THE STAGE OF YOUR BUSINESS

Have you wondered what makes some people dazzling speakers?

I found this to be one of the most intriguing questions not because it is a common question, not because public speaking is an invaluable skill, and not because people find you interesting if you are able to give a speech. It's because it helped me understand who I am from the inside if I could stitch together a story and convey a message to an audience.

It even helps me know that I am understood when I speak.

To get to that point, you have to pass three big stages of evolution as a communicator.

But, let me caution you. You might not find it to be easy. You might not even succeed instantly. You might have upsetting moments when you stall or feel the speech didn't go well. You might even experience disappointment for a few days if you don't carry out the steps in preparing and delivering your speech.

But know that it is within your power to try. That people just like you and me have tried and succeeded. That through your perseverance, actions, your willingness to explore, you will find a brighter tomorrow.

In the first stage, one has to write the speech and deliver it in front of an audience.

However, you might face some difficulties in this stage.

Even though you have a speech, it might not fit in the time you have to deliver it.

That means you have to rehearse the speech after cutting out some content while still delivering the core message. That takes some effort.

Once finished, you deliver the speech. Yet, you find that it could be much better because you have now developed the confidence in speaking in front of a group of people. There is hope for making it even better.

In stage two, you have to review the overall delivery of your speech. Review the structure and the way you connect with the audience. Do you have language that engages them? Is the speech relevant to the audience? Is your opening and closing of the speech delivering impact?

These are the questions you could answer in stage two.

In stage three, you have the chance to use gestures, modulate your voice and transform your speech into an outstanding one. Here, you could create a repeatable and scalable method for this speech and future speeches.

Interestingly, you will have the same opportunity in your business.

The three stages are:

#1 Working in the business

#2 Working on the business

#3 Transforming the business

Let's dive in and see what it means to be working in these three stages of your business. You will find striking likeness.

WORKING IN THE BUSINESS

When you are working in the business, it means you are using existing procedures and methods to deliver goods and services. It also means you are in the day-to-day work in operations and sales.

You find that your teams also continue to carry out your default business strategy.

WORKING ON THE BUSINESS

Here, you are getting a top view of your business. You can review and revise existing procedures and methods to make your operations and sales more effective.

Your teams begin to learn to carry out newer strategies for more business growth and higher efficiencies in the work they do.

TRANSFORMING THE BUSINESS

In transforming the business, you can take the business to a whole new level. What this means is that you have not only improved your procedures and methods, but you've also increased your business value and made the work repeatable and scalable.

It is a transition from a regular business to the next level of becoming a franchise or multi-site company.

THREE LEVELS OF BUSINESS PERFORMANCE

The three levels of business performance are:

#1 Net profit

In this level, your small business could be in creation or disorder or somewhere between.

Your small business focuses here on increasing net profit.

You're in creation when you haven't set up a profitable niche in your target market. You aren't carrying out work against a solid business plan. And you still need to pass breakeven point.

In creation, small businesses are researching the market, modeling the businesses and launching.

You're in disorder when you don't have proper cash flow from your small business. Your small business focuses on creating profitable revenue quickly.

In disorder, small businesses are investing, driving forward and growing.

Every business in this level needs:

- Unique Selling Point
- Current Business Plan
- Breakeven Plan
- Revenue Budget

- Marketing Plan

- Sales Method

- Team Building

#2 Cash flow

In this level, your small business focuses on preserving positive cashflow.

You're here when you have positive cashflow. Many businesses don't make it to this stage. It's also important to keep up positive cashflow.

Some businesses who get to this stage spend unnecessarily and could lose their advantage of positive cashflow. So small businesses must develop methods and teams in this level.

In this level, small businesses are organizing their teams, measuring the business performance and adjusting the business model.

Every business in this level needs:

- Cash Recovery

- Hiring employees

- Assessments

- KPI

- Bonus Plan

#3 Return on investment (ROI)

In this level, your small business is in the prosperity and experiencing freedom or somewhere between the two. Your small business focuses on return on investment, or ROI.

You're in this level when you have managed your profitability. You have real momentum in the market. And the business has a life detached from the small business owner.

You're experiencing freedom when your business creates plenty of free cash flow. And you start to enjoy a quality lifestyle as the business runs with small effort.

In this level, small businesses are creating economies of scale, investing in growth, and repaying debt. Small businesses are reproducing successes by buying new businesses, entering new markets and testing the business leaders. So, the small business owner can now enjoy the harvest of free cashflow and free time. Or even exit the business.

Every business here needs:

- Strategic Plan

- Team Meetings

- Time Recovery

- Organization Structure

- Operations & Training Manual

- Lean Methods

- Delegation Plan

- Leadership Succession

- Exit Plan

SMALL BUSINESS ASSESSMENT

When I start with a new coaching client, one of first steps they take is to finish the small business assessment.

It has about 100 questions in a survey. Typically, business owners finish answering them in about 3 hours.

Once you answer the survey in full, you will get an e-mail with your business performance report and the recommended solutions. It is in a PDF format and will also show your business performance level as described in the previous section.

You could buy the survey at: bit.ly/small-business-evaluation-survey

MAXIMIZING HELP FROM A BUSINESS COACH

There are various stages where you could maximize help from a business coach.

When I first start with my coaching clients, here is what I recommend.

Start:

1. Book a strategy call.
2. Decide on monthly coaching program (Bronze, Silver, Gold or Platinum).
3. Sign coaching agreement & finish Small Business Assessment.
4. Settle coaching agenda and coaching start date.

Ongoing:

5. Keep QBO bookkeeping up-to-date.
6. Enter all details in coaching agenda.
7. Review cloud shared folders for work before coaching session.

8. Read and review all E-books, videos or other shared materials and e-mails before coaching session.

9. Be ready to talk about actions and goals from previous session.

10. Decide on next meeting date.

When we follow these steps and take actions in a disciplined way, you will find outstanding value from the coaching program.

I have helped hundreds of businesses grow substantially in a short period, and I know that you could also find the tools and coaching that I offer to do the same for you and your business.

INCREASING BUSINESS WORTH FOR BEST EXIT STRATEGY

There are many steps you could take as an owner to increase your business worth. However, you should know the stage of your business.

Stage #1: If you are beginning as an entrepreneur where you are researching the market, modeling your business, and launching, then you want to consider developing a unique selling point, a business plan, and figure out your breakeven point.

You want to carry out the strategy to meet or exceed your breakeven point as quickly as possible in this stage.

Stage #2: If you are here, you are probably wanting to become profitable. What it means is that you want more predictable revenue.

This will become possible with revenue budgeting, a marketing plan, a sales management method, and a team building method.

Stage #3: You are now positive in cash flow and want help in investing the cash in proper tools and people. Organize, measure results, and adjust the business model so you have a repeatable procedure for growth.

You want to have cash recovery plans, gather the right employees, assess them, and build a KPI method and bonus plan.

Stage #4: In this stage, your business is running profitably in the market without you having to be there in the business each day.

Here, you will need help with a strategic plan, team meeting philosophy, and time management methods.

Stage #5: Here, your business is having cash surplus, and the business runs with little support from you.

You will need help with a delegation plan, leadership succession, and a business exit procedure.

Working together, we will evaluate your business and carry out the necessary strategies so you increase your business worth. Then you can sell at the highest possible price.

KEY TAKEAWAYS

- Working in the business means default procedures and day-to-day activities.

- Working on the business means getting a helicopter view and improving how you do work.

- Transforming the business means focusing on return on investment in the business.

- Net profit, cash flow, and ROI are three levels of business performance.

- Take the small business assessment to know your business performance level.

- Know the best ways to maximize help from your business coach when you start and when it is ongoing.

- Know where you fit in the 5 business stages so you can take the right steps to increase value.

Chapter 7:

CULTIVATE A
COMPETITIVE MINDSET

If you had any interest in tennis in the '90s, it is difficult for you to have missed watching Pete Sampras at his best.

I admire his game, not for having won so many titles, but because he makes it look effortless.

Obviously, it did not happen overnight. As some commentators put it, "Pete grew his tennis skills brick by brick." Yet, one of the stellar moments in his growth as a tennis player took place when he changed from the two-handed backhand to the one-handed one.

If you read more about it, you will find that Pete wanted to use a one-handed backhand because he wanted to win Wimbledon. That was his long-term goal. Volleying with this type of backhand would give him speed and advantage. That was how he was drastically going to change his game.

A few points to note here. Pete changed his playing style early when he was just 14. Changing later than that would have evaporated the advantage.

Second. This strategy brought out an aggressive serve and volley game. The one-handed backhand aptly complemented this playing style. He took risks, but they were calculated risks.

There is a disruptive strategy in changing to the one-handed backhand. You have to coil your torso in a way that you turn away from your opponent. The greater the turn, the more surreptitious your shot. It will make it difficult for your opponent to anticipate where the ball could land. However, you will feel equally vulnerable when you start playing this way because it won't feel natural. Yet, it is a risk that will pay off big time if you stick with it long-term. That's exactly what happened with Pete.

Five years passed. Sampras became the youngest U.S. open tennis champion ever. Three years later, he won the first Wimbledon title. He then went on to win 14 Grand Slam titles before he retired. Serve-and-volley tennis and precise one-handed backhand volleys embellished his playing style. Others followed his footsteps expecting similar gains.

Cultivating a competitive mindset starts with defining what you will do to reach your eventual goal.

It works the same way in your business.

When you look at your business and you decide you want to become a 20-million-dollar company from a 2-million-dollar company in 5 years, that becomes your goal. You want 10X growth in 5 years. That's what it means.

Ask yourself: "What part of the business will you change that you find uncomfortable today? And that part is the one that is already helping other businesses lead in the industry. Is it AI marketing, is it pricing, or is it something else? Learn to read, research, and apply new strategies that will help you achieve your goal.

When I work with my clients, I want them to know a few things on their way to developing a competitive mindset.

Here are a few items to consider.

BUSINESS COACHING IS NOT A "MAGIC PILL"

You have probably already noticed that I have talked about coaching and its benefits throughout this book. Yet, I want to caution you that business coaching isn't a "magic pill" for business growth. Yes, it will make your journey of growth even more enjoyable when you develop a learning mindset.

Yet, it takes effort.

You have to not only invest more time, but also work towards applying the strategies and align your teams, reduce your costs, and boost your sales at the same time.

It might even feel uncomfortable as you take these steps, much like changing to the one-handed backhand in tennis as we have seen earlier. But know there is light at the end of the tunnel.

You will see the rewards when you achieve your goal. But you have to stick with the plan and believe in your ability to get to your destination.

OVERWHELM FROM STRATEGIES

Even though most business owners who join the coaching program stick with the plan, some feel "burn-out" sooner.

It is not because they aren't having the right mindset, but because they jump from one solution to the next. That leaves a "scatter-brain" approach to applying strategies.

It shows that some don't want to go through the grind in defining the work or doing the work that takes you one step closer to more business growth.

This is what I call "overwhelm from strategies."

The best way to avoid it is to realize that each solution could take three to six months or even longer to fulfill. Acting on more than two solutions at any given time could present a challenge to the business owner who is short on time.

For example, if you are carrying out a solution to craft a unique selling point for your business, you have to finish several steps.

Read the E-book or materials that help you define or customize the USP for your business.

Next, make sure it aligns with your overall business strategy.

Prepare new content.

Once confirmed, use it in different places such as brochures, team meetings, websites, landing pages, and in other relevant areas.

All of this work could take a few months.

UNCOVERING REASONS FOR RETREAT

One reason for retreating from applying business growth strategies comes from underestimating the work you need to prepare and do when you hire a business coach.

Some business owners spend way too much time working in the business. That leaves fewer hours to work on the business.

Others lack staff in the business and that makes them hard pressed for time to work on the business. In such cases, I help business owners prepare a job description and help them hire the right people.

We finish this task after finishing the delegation plan so business owners can transfer non-value tasks to these new resources.

Now, you will be ready to move forward.

ENVISIONING VICTORY

Some of the great tennis players visualize their moves and plays ahead of the game as if they play it on their mind's television.

Similarly successful business owners do the same. They anticipate moves in the industry, market, and make matching moves in their business.

When we work together, business owners improve their skills and competency in applying the right strategies and do it while adapting to their market.

LEVERAGING COACHING

If you are a business owner, how do you leverage coaching?

One of the best ways is to work on the coaching agenda, ask follow-up questions, read study materials, keep accounting books up-to-date, and be ready for the coaching session. Show commitment.

Some business owners want the coach to carry out the solution. They want help at every step of the way but they don't want to take risks. They hesitate because they don't want to make mistakes.

This is a mistake.

Remember. Your business coach is not your business consultant.

Making mistakes and learning from failure is the best way to move forward in the business. There is no solution that solves every business problem without tests and trials. Listen to objective advice. Share your experiences in carrying out strategies. Observe. Adjust and learn to repeat. That will take you further.

As a business coach, I help business owners review various strategies. We work together in a way the strategies have the highest chance of success in your market and industry.

WHAT SUCCESSFUL BUSINESSES DO

Successful CEOs, entrepreneurs, and owners invest in business coaching. They don't procrastinate. They find value in advice and privacy while even working online with a coach. And they recognize the three major benefits from coaching help.

1. Realizing the full potential for your business
2. Applying world-class strategies, tools, and templates
3. Accountability for achieving peak performance

KEY TAKEAWAYS

- Business coaching will help you develop a learning mindset and enjoy growing your business.
- Know the time it takes to carry out solutions so you avoid overwhelm.
- Uncover reasons for not working on the business is part of business coaching.

- Develop a winning mindset and picture victory in the market for your goods and services.
- Know how to leverage coaching and benefit from it.
- Get 3 benefits from coaching and know what successful CEOs do.

Chapter 8:

WHY WORK WITH A BUSINESS COACH?

I could tell you the benefits of working with a coach or mentor. Frankly, I'm doing it all through this book. So, let me do something different.

Sometimes one feels the urge to share a story about someone who had a special skill. That skill helped him become an incomparable coach and mentor.

I was fortunate to know such a person. And that's the story I'm sharing with you here.

Thank you, Virender K Mago, for not only steering me from life's desert but the extraordinary mentorship you showed in guiding me to where I am today.

You must already be thinking, I'm talking to you about someone you don't even know. As a handwriting reader and intuition specialist, VK Mago, as he came to be known, has been an unwavering support in my life. He had unusual abilities to help people improve their lives through better handwriting. He remained a fixture in my life's confusions, guiding me in the darkest hour and through the toughest turbulence. He passed away in 2020 but left behind an indelible memory.

Let's face it. Many of us have or will face a time when you might need closure on the passing of a near relative or friend.

Let me tell you about my rendezvous.

When my father passed away in February of 2014, I wasn't getting closure, even though we were expecting it.

I wanted answers.

That was when I went to Mago. I told him I wanted to know what my father was thinking as he was lying in coma in the hospital. Was he unhappy? What were his last thoughts? What did he want to tell us?

At that moment, Mago paused and said, "'I'm thankful to all. I have no regrets.' That is what I hear from your father, Suresh. That's what he told me," Mago replied.

That stunned me. It made me speechless. I felt like I had just choked. And it was not without reason.

I knew that it was not only how my father would have spoken it, but exactly the way he would have said it. Those were his words, nothing more, nothing less.

So, I'll leave you with a picture that seizes this spirit. It's from that day in 2003, when people queued up for having their signature read, asking Mago 3 questions about their future, marked with the words, "You are what your signature reveals." They were men and women, eager and full of expectations, finally going home knowing a bit more about themselves.

And they were asked what it was like to be read. One of them gave a simple reply: "I want to learn this art and know more about this person." And that was me. We met for the first time. And we were in touch until he passed away from lung failure.

So, I propose a toast: To the person who guided me, to the mentor who shaped my thinking, and to that divine force—that fundamental force—that says no grief is too long, no worry is too great. Through trials, we don't simply endure, we emerge spiritually stronger than ever before, knowing that our brightest days are yet to come, and they shine because of you.

COACHING PRIVACY

One of the best reasons for working with a business coach is privacy.

You will discover that you could have a private one-on-one conversation about your business without ever feeling vulnerable when you talk with your coach. You don't have to hesitate to talk about time, your team, or money in your business.

You know that it isn't helpful talking with your employees about your business issues because they could take the issue differently. You could lose leverage. And there are a host of other reasons you want to keep your business challenges to yourself.

You also know that it is not a good topic to bring up at your dinner table with your family.

That is the reason working with a business coach becomes the obvious choice for CEOs, entrepreneurs and business owners.

Sometimes, business owners even find it difficult to talk with their partners if they have continuing issues.

But let me share this advice. You don't want to treat your business coach as a life coach because their roles are different.

Once you develop rapport, working with a business coach can give you the competitive advantage while preserving the privacy of the business.

RESULTS-ORIENTED APPROACH

Working with a weekly or bi-weekly coaching agenda, I help business owners review their last month's revenues, gross and net margins, leads and sales conversions.

We also look at goals and actions for the month. We set realistic dates and review this separate agenda during each coaching session.

All this work brings a certain rigor in driving the business.

When business owners experience this structure and continuity, they enjoy working on the business and improving their business results.

You will develop new and better habits that help you take decisive actions in your business.

WORLD-CLASS TOOLS, TEMPLATES AND ONLINE STORAGE

When business owners can use world class tools and templates in twenty-one areas of time, teams, and money, we leave no stone unturned.

Whether you are going from net profits to more cash flow or more return on investment, these templates will help you not only measure but also improve your business results.

MORE OBJECTIVITY AND ONE-ON-ONE ONLINE SKYPE SESSIONS

Using Skype sessions, you will find that you don't have to drive around to meet your business coach.

We share common templates, agendas, and tools right online. It saves time and improves productivity in a way unseen before.

When you find online storage as a bonus, it will simplify work and remove the need for unnecessary e-mails to exchange documents.

SKILL DEVELOPMENT AND FLEXIBLE WEEKEND COACHING

Undoubtedly, you will develop new skills and even sharpen most of them when we work together.

When we see the effects of your decisions, month after month, you will find out how to build clarity and be more objective about your business issues.

Whether it is dealing with an employee or changing sales strategies, you will find yourself to be ready.

When I started working first with business owners, I realized that many of them couldn't come out of their business during the day to take part in coaching. They spend their day in operating their company and making sales.

I also found out that most business owners preferred working on their business during the weekends.

That sparked a new idea.

I have now set up coaching sessions on Saturdays and Sundays from 12 to 5 pm. And clients love the new timings. It suits their calendar.

The coaching clients I work with are free from distractions and we are now building their business brick by brick.

LIFT BUSINESS LEVEL

Having a structured small business assessment gives a strong start for business owners.

They no longer have to guess or have abstract advice on their business issues.

Once you take the survey, you will get an invaluable small business evaluation report giving you the current level of your business.

You will see each of the twenty one areas of time, team and money. You will also see your business score not only in each area but also your overall score.

This report in pdf format will even give you solutions for the 21 different challenges of time, team and money in your business.

KEY TAKEAWAYS

- Business coaching helps you explore solutions for business issues in a private setting.
- Build rigor and improve business results from business coaching.
- Take advantage of world-class tools, templates and online storage.
- Experience the convenience and benefits of online business coaching.
- Discover convenient weekend coaching sessions for owners.
- Get the small business evaluation report to assess your business.

Chapter 9:

PUSH THE PEDAL

Did you know CEOs in 2008 and 2009 got an excuse to massively fire thousands of people from their jobs because the economy tanked? Corporatism, the housing boom, the stock market boom–all are over. What that means is that you can't stay in your job for life.

Did you know that since 2009, unemployment is going down, but part-time employment is going up? Research shows Fortune 500 companies are firing people and getting them back as part-timers, demoting them in some way.

But here's the good news.

Innovation is bringing more solo entrepreneurs in America. If you ever dreamed of becoming an entrepreneur, this is the time. Seize the moment. It is yours.

Research shows older workers experience turbulence regardless of income, education, geography or industry. More than 50% of workers with high school education face damaging layoffs or involuntary separation when they cross their fifties after years of steady jobs. More education is hardly a shield: 55% of those with college or graduate degrees experience similar job losses.

Some years back, I read about Paul. Paul was a janitor at a school. Paul made many friends through his hard work at the school. He kept the floors spic and span.

The school principal walked up to Paul one day and said: "Paul, I know you have been working here for 30 years, and I thank you for your tireless service. But we have a new policy. All workers must have a high school diploma, and I know you don't have one. So, I'm sorry to tell you that your work at the school ends today."

Paul: "I'm shocked. What am I supposed to do?"

Principal: "We will pay you for six months' severance, Paul, but that's the best we can do. I'm sorry, Paul."

Paul: "I understand. I've faced changes in my life before. I'll get through this one too."

Paul came home sad. But he didn't sulk for long. He reached out to all the people he knew and asked them for small cleaning jobs. People gave him work. Soon he earned enough to start his own cleaning company.

One day the Vice President of his bank invited Paul to speak with him about his loan application.

He said, "Paul, I've never seen you before. You're such a successful business owner. If you just sign here, we'll proceed with your business loan."

At that moment, Paul replied, "I don't know how to sign. Would it be okay if I marked an X?"

The bank's VP, looking over Paul's shoulder, whispered, "If only you had a college education, imagine how far you could have gone."

To that Paul quickly replied, "If I would have had that, I'd still be a janitor at the school, not a business owner."

In the end, that is the condition for all of us. It is our calling from above; the belief that becoming an entrepreneur has rewards; the belief that this is another call for personal freedom; the belief that each one of us is at the fork on the road today. I believe we can each rise to our highest potential. I believe that as we stand at this fork, we can make the right choice and dare to differ from someone else deciding how much they should pay us.

Here's my question for you: Do you want to stop some big monopoly from deciding your fate? Do you want to stop someone else from putting a price tag on your head? Do you want to take your chances and own them?

Then become an entrepreneur.

But let me warn you. You might not succeed overnight. You might not enjoy the perks. You might not have the same income. But what you'll have is something far more worthy—the pleasure of pursuing your passion.

OVERCOMING HESITANCY

Some business owners are willing to work on the business.

They see value. Yet they hesitate because they doubt their ability to succeed. They equally fear failure.

Here is what I have to tell them.

I'm here to help you carry out your strategies for business growth—week after week. I'm committed to your success.

Remember, I have overcome exactly the same doubts you have and the same fears you have of failure. I have used world-class tools and templates proved to help thousands of other businesses get ahead.

When you work with me, you will have someone experienced and committed to help you succeed in growing your business.

Note that most business owners already had overcome their procrastination when I asked them this question.

"Does growing your business by getting help from a business coach work for you or not? What would you like to do?"

If you are on the fence about business coaching, ask yourself: Do I want to risk doing nothing?

The answer will tell you if you are okay with the status quo. If the answer is no, then move forward with business coaching.

TIME TO GROW IS NOW

Is it the right time to grow your business? You might get the answer if you told yourself these two things.

It is okay to keep this problem in business growth. Many business owners do. But it is also okay to fix the problem now, while I can help as a business coach.

When the economy is shaky, it is a great time to cut costs and the more skilled you become in this area, the more you will learn to grow your profits. That's a given.

You could cut fixed costs first and then variable costs. Either way, you have opportunities. Use a revenue and profit budget, a cash gap plan, and a lean manufacturing method to cut your costs.

These are just a few examples.

In all cases, you will get templates and guidance in reducing costs in your business. That's what happens when you work with a business coach.

Once you carry out this strategy, we will work together to see how it is helping you increase your business profits.

HARNESSING NEW SKILLS

Research shows that key new skills are becoming more elusive. It is not only affecting business owners but also the people you have to bring on board to solve those pressing business issues.

Some business owners instantly find business coaching as the best conduit to advance their skills in the business.

It is not because they don't already have some of it today but because there is much more out there that you still need to learn.

If you notice in the last five years, there have been different ways to attract buyers using automated marketing funnels. This is just one such technology and its transformation. There are so many more like this one.

When you want to improve KPIs, we are talking about people taking ownership and then helping grow the business. You also need the right people in the right jobs.

That comes with acquiring the right people with the right skills in your industry. You start with a job description and then pick the channels to find people.

In some cases, business owners want customized training on a sales management tool, such as Pipedrive or even an e-mail marketing platform such as Mailchimp, Mautic, or Constant Contact.

Since I offer a one-stop shop for business services, I offer custom training in all of these areas including sales and marketing.

I go further and build 3-page or 5-page websites inside a week.

These are professional websites with domain, hosting, and even maintenance and support.

APPLYING STRATEGIES

Let's face it. There are two main strategies in any business. Your business is using either a cost-based or value-based strategy.

Most business owners find themselves doing all the work themselves in the business. It is not because they want to but because they don't find it easy to transfer the work or trust someone else to do it as well as they could.

This is where the "perfection" mindset steps in. You then have to ask yourself: "How long do I want to continue doing everything in the business without asking for help?" The answer will lead you to the next step.

In this example, it is best to transfer the work using a delegation plan. For example, I help the business owner go through four stages of transferring work so you could do it correctly. I know this has come up before because it affects time, the team, and money.

There are 20 other areas, where we will work together to help you grow your business.

BUILD REPEATABLE PROCEDURES

What value do "repeatable procedures" have in your business? If you ask me, I'd say it has a ton of value in my business.

This is another side-benefit from business coaching.

When I work with clients, I give them a template to add procedures to their operations and training manual. This could include pictures, videos and content. You hold one person accountable to collect the content and update the steps. And you do it for each job in your business.

The purpose is to help new employees come up to speed with their work when they have to follow a manual and do their job, step by step. Such measures not only save time but build confidence in your business teams to quickly become productive.

COMPANY-WIDE TRAINING

The best way to influence your business growth is also to offer company-wide training to your team.

What are some of the training workshops that influence business growth?

- Team building and harmony
- Sales management method
- Applying and utilizing Customer Relationship Method (CRM) tools
- Carrying out strategic plan

Once you have your team building and harmony workshop, your team will discover new ways of working together.

Each team member will go through an assessment. What this means is that you reduce conflicts because they now understand each other's communicating style based on the assessment. That's the advantage in holding this workshop.

A workshop on the sales management method will enable your sales team to work through their weaknesses and follow a repeatable and scalable method to grow sales.

I have also held workshops for a sales CRM such as Pipedrive. Such a platform helps sales teams make the best use of sales tools because they will discover how to capture leads, track communications, follow up, and advance the sale through various stages.

A team workshop for the strategic plan will outline the mission, vision, and core values of your team so they pull the whole company forward together.

KEY TAKEAWAYS

- Learn what it takes to avoid procrastination.
- Working with a business coach will produce benefits in any economy.
- Know that business coaching helps to harness new skills.
- Before applying know the two broad business strategies.
- Know what it means to build repeatable business procedures.
- Know how business growth comes from coaching and company-wide training.

Chapter 10:

WHAT NEXT?

You are at the brink of more excitement. Your journey doesn't end here.

You have experienced what it takes to work with a business coach and create value for your business. That means you have increased your business value so you could command the best price when you are ready to sell.

You have to answer the question about why anyone would want to buy your business. There are also three methods of finding your business worth.

- Using 5 years of cash flow
- Using company location
- Using market demand for the type of business

Sometimes businesses may have existing buyers inside the company. Other times, one has to set the price and advertise in the market to get buyers. Either way, you will need other alliances to prepare the business for sale.

The second phase is to protect value of your business. That means you work with your accountant for tax-related help and file accordingly.

The third phase is to compound value of your business. That means you work with your finance advisor and multiply your wealth from the business.

Finally, you spread value. That means working with attorneys and ironing out patents and copyrights for your goods and services.

LEVERAGING GROWTH

Once your business grows and you are producing enough independent streams of income, you could create separate profit and loss units of the business.

You could then also have independent teams preserving profits for these units.

These steps will leverage the growth of your business.

MORE INCOME STREAMS

With proper coaching and growth, you could have some passive and active streams of income. These would act on top of your core business activity.

That means that you will have the flexibility to achieve the revenue and profit goals beyond the original track for your business.

LEADERSHIP HANDOFF PLAN

If you have already increased the value of your business, it is time for you to have a succession plan in place.

Think about the plan you will have in place to grow your management team. Think also about ensuring long-term commitment and any profit-sharing plan you propose.

That means making a key leader report to you. There are a few steps to find, empower and develop a leader.

If you're ready for a succession plan, here's what happens. With the delegation plan you will now only review KPIs, reports, and forecasts coming from your team. No other work on your part. Your time becomes even more important.

One has to ask what leadership influence you have around your company.

You will find the best leadership successor when he focuses on respect and sets up exemplary work. What that means is the one whom people follow for what they are and what they represent and what they have done for their followers.

EXIT PLAN

When we work together, our goal is to help you create a sellable business which works without you. That means you already know why someone would want to buy your business right now.

You will be slowly becoming a high caliber leader so you have a team help you run your business. That shows you now have the time to become an investor in the business. Your money is now working for you.

Then you're ready for a role as an entrepreneur.

Using certain tools such as LivePlan, I help owners review their financial ratios and compare them with competitors in the same industry and zip code.

When owners want to sell their business, I help them through coaching to increase their profits so their business can get a better price. Connecting with intermediaries, we bring a new method to selling your business.

INTERNATIONAL INFLUENCE

We have focused on expanding your business and growing it in the United States. Once you reach the stage of ROI improvement, you will find a myriad of opportunities if you are seeking further to expand abroad.

These are some of the other areas we could explore through coaching.

KEY TAKEAWAYS

- Know how to leverage business growth once you're there.
- Know how to explore more income streams.
- Set up leadership succession so you can exit the business.
- Know how to carry out the exit plan.
- What about going international with your business?

CONCLUSION

There are two types of business owners in this world.

Type #1: Those who work on the business as a part-time exercise. They do it all themselves. They love the added responsibility. They also want to show their employees that they want to simplify life at work for everyone. And some of their procedures may even do it.

Type #2: Those that work with a business coach. They love building their business brick by brick. And instead of ad-hoc activity, they take **regular action**. They willingly invest their time, money, and energy into growing their business.

Which type are you?

As business owners we can easily grow our business when we know the full stretch of the business, get access to world-class tools and templates and when we achieve our peak potential because someone keeps us accountable.

That is what you get in business coaching.

Now, you have a better understanding of how to work with a business coach. You have the building blocks to make your business grow in the shortest time.

MOST GRATEFUL

I'm most grateful that you bought this book and read it.

Could I ask you for a favor? It would help others decide on buying their next book if you could leave an honest review for this book online.

I wish you the greatest success in your business growth.

ABOUT THE AUTHOR

Suresh Iyengar is a Profitability Coach who collaborates with CEOs, entrepreneurs, executives and business owners to uncover hidden profits and create new wealth from private profitability coaching.

After spending nearly two decades in multi-million dollar companies, Suresh knows exactly what drives business growth, profits and sales—and it's not abstract ideas. It's how you craft your detailed plan and carry it out, quickly building loyal fans for your goods and services.

Suresh has written over 100 blog articles and published 12 Amazon eBooks on business growth.

Suresh is a versatile public speaker and Toastmasters Advanced Communicator Silver, Intuit Proadvisor and LivePlan Expert Advisor, helping businesses experience explosive growth using advanced solutions in the areas of time, team and money.

On getting promoted to a top PMO leadership role in a Fortune 500 company, Suresh drove business efficiency that increased order ability 43% and cut costs $214M. As a result, the company grew profits 30% in 8 months—despite relentless order intake. Earned ABB Quality Salute award for business unit performance.

Suresh coached executives and business units in 80 countries.

Suresh has a bachelor's degree in Instrumentation Technology, master's degree in Electrical Engineering and MBA. He is a Professional Engineer, Project Management Professional and Stanford University certified in project management

Why Suresh? Other professionals tell you how quickly they can help you grow your business, but what they don't tell you is that they give broad roadmaps and no detailed solutions. They charge for every small abstract advice. And they don't offer a complete solution that delivers results. Business owners are tired of working in this way. Suresh takes the time to craft a full solution that's detailed and works for YOU.